GLEN DO YOU EVER LOOK OUT AT THE CITY AND THINK?
ABOUT WHAT! HOW BLACK IT WOULD BE IF ALL THE LIGHTS WENT OUT!

NO! HOW THERE IS SOMEONE FOR EVERYONE!

WE NEED LOTS OF PRAISE:

"Buckle your seatbelts, nerds and gay metal heads. Your joyride awaits."
- Queer Sighted

"Henry and Glenn Forever brought me to my knees, bent me over and procured a unicorn from my privatest parts"
- Jeanne Fury, Decibel

"More than a political statement, this looks like a fun fantasy where Danzig and Rollins are an out and proud - but hardcore - Burt and Ernie."
- Bitch Magazine

"It plays into the inherent homoeroticism of early mosh-pit man piles, but it also acknowledges that just as fans are at the mercy of our idols' creative whims, musical heroes and legends are also subject to the imaginations of the listeners."
- Carrie Brownstein, NPR

"The Comics wizards at Igloo Tornado have proven what the rest of us only suspected: Henry & Glenn are two great tastes that taste great together. Like peanut butter and jelly. Or poppers and cherry lube. I hope it really does last forever."
- J. Bennett, Decibel

"We can't believe it- there's finally an object in the world that Carrie Brownstein and J. Bennett can agree on!"
- The Boston Phoenix

"A long running fantasy of mine finally realized in comic form! Henry and Glenn Forever gives me the warm fuzzies in all the wrong places."
- Ed Luce, creator of Wuvable Oaf Comics

"You know why I am depicted in a comic? Because I am fuckin' famous."
-Henry

Henry + Glenn = 4-Ever

by

Igloo Tornado

thank you joe

cantankerous titles
po box 14332
portland, or 97293
cantankeroustitles.com

cantankerous titles #7
isbn 978-1-934620-93-9

Dedicated to Henry and Glenn

You have always been an inspiration.

Please don't punch us in the face.

We love you.

So, what's this book all about?

Henry and Glenn are very good "friends."
They are also "room mates."
Daryl and John live next door.
They are satanists.

That's all you need to know.

REPEAL PROP H8
NO CAN DO!
OH! I CAN'T GO FOR THAT!

DO THESE PANTS MAKE MY BUTT LOOK FAT?
YES.
TOMN! '05

Dear Diary,

i wish i could suppress my feelings like a Vulcan. but i'm more like a werewolf full of untamed emotion, always on edge and ready to fight. i yelled at Henry the other day because he never does the dishes and i always end up being the one who cleans up after him. i wanna help him because he's so busy ~~[illegible]~~ getting ready for his tour, but i'm so overwhelmed. i can't keep up with everything. i can't be the only one who

YOU NEED THERAPY... NOT!
MY SONGS

11-08-08

Dear Henry,

I've been reading Glenn's diary again...
I should spend some more time with him.
Why am I writing to myself in the third person? I hate myself sometimes...

IN HINDSIGHT, MAYBE WE SHOULD HAVE JUST GOTTEN TATTOOS.

NOW PUT ON THIS HORSE SUIT AND I'LL RIDE YOU OVER TO DARYL & JOHN'S HALLOWEEN PARTY.
BUT I THOUGHT WE WERE GONNA BE...
PONCH AND JOHN THIS YEAR.

OK, Now roll for your mana points.
I'm not rolling shit until you let me wear your hat.
DRAGON MASTERZ

HEY LOVERBOY NEXT TIME USE TOILET PAPER!

PUT YOUR SHIRT ON, PLEASE...

HI MR. SAD-MUFFIN, WHAT TIME IS IT?
IT'S PUPPET PLAY-TIME!

HEY HALL IT'S PARYLL, I FOUND A GREAT APARTMENT, EXCEPT
THERE ARE THESE TWO GUYS ONE LITTLE GUY AND A RATHER
LARGE OAF. I THINK THEY ARE A LITTLE MORE THEN ROOMATES
BUT THEY KEEP THE GARDEN NICE, ANYWAYS SEE YOU AT
THE SEANCE LATER TONIGHT

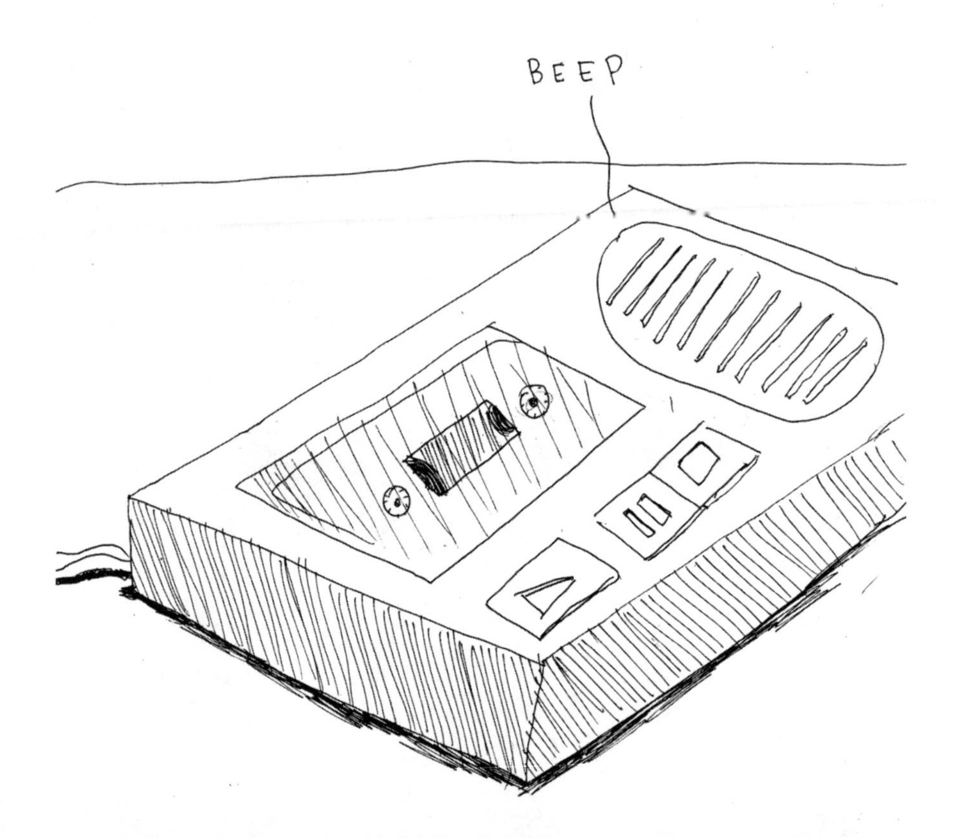

HEY GLENN, I THINK OUR NEW NEIGHBORS ARE SATANISTS!
I'M SCARED!

CAN WE PAINT THE BEDROOM BLACK THIS WEEKEND?
WHY DOES EVERYTHING HAVE TO BE BLACK?
TOMN! '05

dear diary,

i've been thinking about starting a new band. i was thinking i mite try doing a black metal band because it seems like that's what the kids are into these days. i was trying out some corpse-paint ideas in the bathroom this mourning and HENRY said "WHAT THE HELL ARE YOU DOING?! YOU SHOULD JUST BE YOUR SELF!" i got really mad at him and we had a fight. but i think really i'm just mad at myself 'cause i don't know who i am anymore... when i look at myself in the mirror

DEAR HENRY,

HOW ARE YOU? THE TOUR IS
GOING OK. I MISS YOU AND
THE DOG SO MUCH. GIVE HER A KISS FOR ME.
YESTERDAY THIS LEAD SINGER
SLAPPED ME, IT HURT SO MUCH
I WISH YOU WERE THERE TO
HAVE HELD ME. WELL I HAVE
TO GO THERE IS A GREAT
DOCUMENTRY ON ABOUT WEREWOLVES.

MISS YOU,

GLENN

XOXOX

HENRY
666 SHADY TREE LN.
LOS ANGELES, CA 90057

I'M PRETTY SURE MR. T WANTS HIS NECKLACES BACK.
ME TOO.

DOES MY BUTT LOOK FAT IN THESE PANTS?
YES.

SO YOU THINK YOUR GONNA LIVE YOUR LIFE ALONE IN DARKNESS AND SECLUSION
I'M DESPERATE AND I NEED HUMAN CONTACT YOUR PERFECT IN EVERYWAY

GLENN,
YOUR SISTER
CALLED SHE SAID
YOU NEED TO
CALL THE DOCTORS
ABOUT INCEMINATION
THEY DONT THINK
IT WORKED

HENRY

SHOEZ MAKE THE MAN
WORD

IS THAT WHAT YOU'RE WEARING?! WE'RE GOING TO DINNER WITH MY MOTHER YOU COULD AT LEAST PUT ON SOME SHOES!
BUT I DON'T HAVE ANY.
TOMN! '05

MOTHERRR...
TATOO

DARYLL,
CAN YOU TALK TO
HENRY AND GLENN WHEN
YOU GET HOME. THEY
ARE VERY UPSET THEIR
DOG IS MISSING.
SEE YOU AT THE
SACRAFICE TONIGHT.
JOHN

"WHEN ANGELS GET TIRED THEY SIT AND REST ON SOFT PILLOWS OF CLOUDS IN THE SKY."

dear diary,

i've been wasting too much time on twitter again. but sometimes i get so lonely when Henry's away. i don't know what to do anymore. i feel so alone. Lost... i keep trying to write some new songs, and i even jammed with Daryl and John in their garage last nite. but when i came home to an empty house all i wanted to do was eat a whole tub of mint-chocolate chip ice cream and watch reruns of the Golden Girls.

BECAUSE YR KISS IS ON MY LIST!

IF I WASN'T SO INTO MYSELF I MIGHT HAVE TIME TO SPEND WITH SOMEONE WHO CARES WHAT I SAY OR DO.
ME TOO

HENRY + GLENN
WE GOT MARRIED IN A FEVER HOTTER THEN A PEPPER SPROUT!
GOIN TO
ACKSON
KEY OF D MINOR
WOLFS
BLOOD

HEY JOHN,
THE NEIGHBORS WANT US TO COME
OVER FOR DINNER AND TO WATCH THE
L WORD I WAS THINKING YOU COULD
MAKE THAT KILLER DEVIL'S FOOD CAKE TO
BRING. BY. SEE YOU AT THE CHAPEL
LATER. OH THERE STILL LOOKING
FOR THEIR DOG

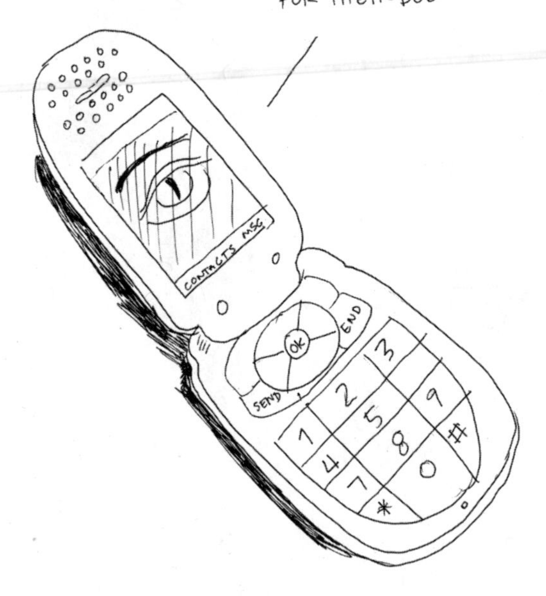

I'VE GOT SOMETHING TO SAY...

COLOR ME BADD
ME TOO

HA HA! I WATCHED THAT MOVIE LAST NIGHT!

dear diary of the dead,

HENRY'S on tour again. i've been feeling kinda down... but Daryl came over last nite and brought some pizza and zombie movies to cheer me up. he's so cool. we had so much fun! he even braided my hair while we watched RETURN OF THE EVIL DEAD!!! i gotta go now. John is holding a seance tonight to try and talk to Jimi. Daryl said i could join them. i wanna get a new outfit to wear, so i'm off to the mall for a shopping spree at Hot topic!!! ♡♡♡

MOMMY CAN I GO OUT AND KILL TONIGHT?
YES "NORMAN", WHATEVER YOU WANT... NOW "MOMMY" HAD A LONG DAY AND JUST WANTS TO RELAX. NOW RUN ALONG AND PLAY OUTSIDE.

HENRY & GLEN

HENRY DO YOU THINK MY BUTT LOOKS FAT IN THESE PANTS?

NOT AT ALL GLEN IN FACT...

CAN YOU HELP TOSS MY SALAD.

I ♥ UNICORNS
ME TOO

I WISH I WERE A UNICORN OF DEATH
ME TOO

HENRY + GLENN

HENRY CAN WE TAKE THESE OLD RECORDS TO THE ANTIQUE'S ROADSHOW FOR PBS

WAY AHEAD OF YOU IM BRINGING THESE BOOKS

OBSCURE RECORDS

LONE WOLF

BLOOD

WOLES

SCARY BOOKS

I'M THE KING OF THE WORLD!

I HATE MYSELF FOR YOU!
I LOVE YOU.

07-08-08

Dear Henry,

It's been a while since I wrote in this diary for a while because I still think it's stupid. But my shrink thinks I need to get more in touch with my emotions. Whatever... I don't know what to do anymore. The radio show is fun. And I guess I still like doing the spoken word tours. But I feel like I'm losing it. I feel like

FUCK THIS

ROCKY HORROR IS PLAYING AT THE NUART HOW ABOUT IT!
YOU KNOW THOSE FISHNETS DONT FIT ME ANYMORE!

dear diary,

i saw a dead bird on the sidewalk while i was walking the dog and it reminded me of how cruel this world is and how at any moment we could be crushed by some unstoppable force and we'll be extinguished forever... forgotten... gone... dead. i'm so glad i get to spend my short life here with Henry. i must find a way to become a werewolf so i can live forever and Henry can be one too. i've read all the books, but

I DON'T HAVE TIME FOR LITTLE COMICS; I'M TOO BUSY LISTENING TO MYSELF TALK ABOUT ME
ME TOO

I WRITE THE SONGS THAT MAKE THE WHOLE WORLD SING. I WRITE THE SONGS I WRITE THE SONGS
I BOUGHT THAT JUICER YOU WANTED ALSO GOT TOILET PAPER

I SAID I'M SORRY...
ARE YOU COMING TO BED?
I'VE GOT A SIX-PACK AND I DON'T NEED YOU!
BEER
BEE

I THINK THAT HUEY LEWIS IS TOTALLY UNDERRATED.
ME TOO

DID I SAY HUEY LEWIS? I MEANT EMMANUEL LEWIS.

ME TOO

Dear Henry,

I should stop reading Glenn's diary. And I should stop stealing paper from it for my own diary. He might notice I'm been reading all of his private thoughts about werewolves and Hitler. He writes about him so much I'm almost jealous... seriously I think he's obsessed. Our therapist says I'm making progress

I'VE GOTTA GET UP EARLY TOMORROW TO GO TAPE THAT VH1 SPECIAL ON HAIR-METAL.
HOW COME VH1 NEVER CALLS ME?
WOLVERINE
TOMN! '05

DEAR GLENN,

THE SPOKEN WORD TOUR IS SO AWESOME. SO MANY GREAT PEOPLE HAVE COME OUT FOR THE READINGS AND THE RESPONSE HAS BEEN SO WONDERFUL. IT'S GREAT THAT ALL THESE PEOPLE STILL WANT TO SEE ME. THEY YELL FOR ME TO DO SOME SONGS WHICH IS GREAT IT MAKES ME FEEL SO GOOD INSIDE

HENRY

GLENN
666 SHADYTREE LN.
LOS ANGELES, CA 90057

09-23-08

Dear Henry,

You are an ASSHOLE!

you stupid Liar.

FUCK YOU!

xxoo

Henry

p.s. diaries are still LAME!

FILL IN YOUR OWN JOKE IF YOU THINK YOU'RE SO DAMN FUNNY

deary diary,

today was a good day! Henry and i had an all day date. we went to the museum and saw some dinosaur bones. and then we had a picnic at the beach!!! ♡♡♡ after our picnic we lifted some weights together. i love to get pumped with Henry!!! but now i'm sad because Henry is leaving tomorrow moorning to shoot some slasher movie. i wish i could act so i could be in a horror movie.

T.V. PARTY TONIGHT!
T.V. PARTY TONIGHT!
T.V. PARTY TONIGHT!
SEX IN THE CITY
GOLDEN GIRLS

HENRY
GLENN

love is...

... an ordinary kind of little angel fuck.

Igloo Tornado
7th Period

Our Ethos

Igloo Tornado is a very good art collective. It is a collected group of art and artists, collecting our thoughts and our art. We drink a lot of beer. Igloo Tornado is with Scot Nobles, Tom Neely, , and Gin Stevens. They do a lot of things.

First of all we are really collected with each other. Like I did drawings and they said it was really good so we all really know what we're talking about. Tom has a lot of cool toys and has an arcade cabinet but he doesn't play a lot and we talk about a lot of movies alot. Things that are awesome are what we like. We like them because they are cool and also we like alot of music like heavy metal and other kinds of music too. We go to Tom's house alot and sometimes Scot's but has a cat and Tom and Scot are allergic and Gin has a cat too. Igloo Tornado is a collective of artists.

Second, we drink some many amounts of beer. One time I brought some zima and the guys made fun of me and they didn't like the zima but I took a chance and I think it was okay after that. Scot has really nice beer glasses but at Tom's we just drink it from the bottle. I haven't been to Gins apartment but I don't think he has glasses either. Sometimes I buy good beer like "Negro Modelo" and sometimes I get Budweiser but a lot of times I forget to bring beer because I don't have it on my mind. I don't bring zimas anymore.

Finally we are 4 people Scot, Tom, , and Gin. We do a lot of different kinds of pictures and drawings and paintings and things but sometimes we do stuff together and we talk a lot about things and we are friends. We like comics and movies. Sometimes some of us make comics, and we make books together and even sell them. We might get swords soon.

In Conclusion, Igloo Tornado is pretty good and hopefully you will see them soon!

www.iglootornado.com